POP CULTURE
REVOLUTIONS

PLAY IT LOUD!

The Rebellious History of Music

by Sara Gilbert

Content Adviser: Jeff Kryka. M.A., Instructor, Department of Music,
University of California, Los Angeles

Reading Adviser: Alexa L. Sandmann, Ed.D., Professor of Literacy,
College and Graduate School of Education, Health, and Human Services, Kent State University

COMPASS POINT BOOKS
a capstone imprint

Compass Point Books
151 Good Counsel Drive
P.O. Box 669
Mankato, MN 56002-0669
www.capstonepub.com

 This book was manufactured with paper containing
at least 10 percent post-consumer waste.

Managing Editor: Catherine Neitge
Designer: Veronica Bianchini
Photo Researcher: Eric Gohl
Library Consultant: Kathleen Baxter
Production Specialist: Jane Klenk

Library of Congress Cataloging-in-Publication Data
Gilbert, Sara.
  Play it loud! : the rebellious history of music / by Sara Gilbert.
    p. cm.—(Pop culture revolutions)
  Includes bibliographical references and index.
  ISBN 978-0-7565-4243-6 (library binding)
  1. Music—Social aspects—Juvenile literature. 2. Music—History and
criticism—Juvenile literature. I. Title. II. Series.
  ML3928.G55 2010
  780.9—dc22   2009030752

Image Credits ©: Alamy: The London Art Archive, 6, The Print Collector, 10; AP Images:
Doug Pizac, 38; Corbis: Neal Preston, 51, 56; DVIC/NARA, 49; Getty Images: Blank
Archives, 59, *Evening Standard*, 22, *Express* Newspapers, 35, FilmMagic/Gary Miller, 44,
FilmMagic/Jeff Kravitz, Frank Driggs Collection, 24, Frank Micelotta, 48, Imagno, 8, 31,
Kevin Winter, 19, Metronome, 13, Michael Ochs Archives, 16, 36, Michael Ochs Archives/
Al Pereira, 33, Michael Ochs Archives/Alice Ochs, 32, Redferns/Ebet Roberts, 37,
Redferns/GAB Archive, 15, 58, Redferns/Janette Beckman, 39, Redferns/Suzie Gibbons,
47, Roger Viollet Collection, 42, Tim Mosenfelder, 26, 52, Time Life Pictures/Charles
Trainor, 28, Time Life Pictures/Thomas D. McAvoy, 34, WireImage/Al Pereira, 29; Landov
LLC/MCT/*Detroit Free Press*/Tony Spina, 30; Library of Congress, 18, 23, 25, 46, 50;
National Archives and Records Administration, 4; Newscom/AFP Photo, 45; Shutterstock:
Adam J. Sablich, 57, Amy K Planz, background (cover and interior), Amy Nichole Harris,
27, Arman Zhenikeyev, cover, 1, background (interior), ayakovlev.com, 40, Christopher
Ewing, back cover (front), 55, Derrick Salters, 20, Kundra, back cover (back), background
(interior), M.E. Mulder, 17.

Printed in the United States of America in Stevens Point, Wisconsin.
122010
006019R

ABLE OF CONTENTS

Sound Track to Change

There's a battle outside
And it is ragin'.
It'll soon shake your windows
And rattle your walls
For the times they are
a-changin'.

—Bob Dylan, "The
Times They Are
A-Changin'"

Joan Baez and Bob Dylan sang from Dylan's *The Times They Are A-Changin'* album during the turbulent 1960s.

Bob Dylan wrote the words of "The Times They Are A-Changin'" in 1963, in the midst of great social and political upheaval in the United States. But his lyrics could also speak to many other eras in history.

Music has long provided the sound track to social, political, and cultural change. Its creators have been known as leaders of their generations. Often they first had to fight for acceptance, though. Many composers who have tried new styles have been rejected and ridiculed; singers who have sung controversial lyrics have often faced angry protests. Even new rhythms, new instruments, and new sounds have sometimes been shunned.

But despite criticism, musicians from Mozart to Marilyn Manson have not given up easily. They have refused to conform to social norms. They have tested the limits with their words and their music. And they have changed not only the popular music of the day but also the world they lived in. And guess what—this pop culture revolution is still happening! Curious? Just turn the page. …

CHAPTER 1

The Movements

People have been making music since humans appeared on Earth. A prehistoric bone flute with five finger holes was recently discovered in Germany, evidence that even during the Stone Age, people liked making music and probably enjoyed listening to others make it.

A 16th century painting reflected music in daily life.

Throughout recorded history, new musical movements have heralded times of social, political, or cultural change. Some movements have fizzled out fast. Others have stood the test of time, sometimes for centuries.

EARLy EXPRESSIONS

The 1300s were not a great time to be alive in Europe. Long, catastrophic wars killed millions, exhausted resources, and destroyed families. The Black Death added more millions to the toll. Although some people, including traveling musicians, created nonreligious music, the Catholic Church controlled the social and cultural climate. The church set rules not only about how to behave but also about what kind of music to play and listen to—mostly vocal chants with one melody line.

Out of that unsettled atmosphere was born the Renaissance, a period in which more creative music began to appear. New stringed instruments, including the viol, an ancestor of the cello, joined the improved brass and wind instruments being used. Then came Johannes Gutenberg's printing press in 1450. In addition to books, the presses made printed music more available and less expensive. Music became part of everyday life for many people. No longer was it reserved for holy days and church services.

The Renaissance was followed by the Baroque era, a time of extremely decorative art and architecture. Musical compositions were elaborately arranged, dramatic, and highly emotional. Then came the Age of Enlightenment, which emphasized knowledge, truth, and freedom—and rejected religion as a primary guiding principle. The leaders of the Enlightenment believed that art, including music, was meant for the masses, not just the ruling class. Out of that belief grew musical works that were logical and balanced, yet simple enough to be enjoyed by the working class. Symphony orchestras combined the sounds of many instruments, adding depth and complexity to compositions.

The Age of Enlightenment, which included the Classical era, was followed by the Romantic era of music. Some of the most renowned composers of all time were part of those two eras—Wolfgang Amadeus Mozart and Franz Joseph Haydn in the Classical period, and Franz Schubert in the Romantic. Ludwig van Beethoven bridged the two eras. Most composers since then have considered that handful of musical geniuses as the masters—but few are content to simply imitate them. Contemporary classical musicians, including the modernist Elliott Carter, have been influenced by their work but continue to integrate new sounds, instruments, and technologies into their compositions. Even today classical music continues to evolve and to take on unique shapes and sounds.

Painter William Hogarth's *Southwark Fair* captured the musical festivities at a popular gathering in 1733.

MUSICAL ERAS

450 to 1450 **Medieval**	Marked by two main styles: monophonic, a simple form with long, flowing melodies of either voices or instruments; and polyphonic, in which rhythms are varied and there is more than one part.
1450 to 1600 **Renaissance**	Composers embraced smooth, gentle rhythms that could be sung or played by groups of like-sounding voices or instruments.
1600 to 1750 **Baroque**	Musicians experimented with ornate melodies, freely mixing voices and instruments.
1750 to 1825 **Classical**	In the midst of the Industrial Revolution and the Enlightenment, musicians returned to simple textures and melodies and often incorporated the piano in their compositions.
1825 to 1900 **Romantic**	New instruments, including winds, are introduced, and longer, more dramatic melodies with full, often dissonant harmonies are common.
1900 to present **Modern**	Huge advances in technology lead to the birth of sound recording and a widening gap between popular music and more artistic music. New instruments and new sounds are introduced.

A watercolor folk painting, *The Old Plantation*, from about 1790 depicted slaves dancing to music derived from Africa. The women are playing a Sierra Leone gourd rattle.

GETTING THE BLUES

The first hint of the blues may have been heard on ships crossing the Atlantic Ocean to North and South America starting in the 16th century. The slaves on the ships had only their voices and the beat in their feet to remind them of home. The tradition of vocal storytelling through music was passed from generation to generation during the more than 200 years of American slavery. Eventually this storytelling evolved into a new form of music. When the enslaved people were granted their freedom during the Civil War, they finally could share their musical expressions publicly.

In the late 1800s, one of those expressions appeared in the form of ragtime. This music, with its syncopated marching beat, was as much fun for musicians to play as for audiences to hear. Although the American Federation of Musicians tried to ban ragtime music in

1901, the bouncy, irresistibly danceable music became increasingly popular in dance halls across the United States—especially in New Orleans, Louisiana.

Ragtime wasn't the only African-American music alive and kicking. Even as that bouncy beat was charming listeners, black musicians in the Mississippi Delta were developing the blues. Blues lyrics often told a sad story, but the music usually made listeners feel better, not worse. "The blues did not come from books," said W.C. Handy, a musician who helped popularize the blues in the early 1900s. "Suffering and hard luck were the midwives that birthed these songs. The blues were conceived in aching hearts."

There's no question that the roots of the blues go all the way back to Africa. And there's also no doubt that its development was uniquely American. The blues became the base from which other musical forms—including jazz and rock 'n' roll—were born.

Born of Slavery

Although the Africans who were shipped to the Americas as slaves starting in the 16th century were forced to leave much behind, they brought their musical traditions with them.

Their powerful rhythms and emotional vocal music had a great influence on the evolution of American music. As the enslaved people labored in the fields, they supported each other with call-and-response work songs. As they rested, they consoled themselves with soulful spirituals. Their music set the stage for both jazz and blues—which in turn influenced many modern musicians. Rocker Peter Gabriel said, "Part of what we consider our fundamental rock and roll heritage originated in Africa. Period."

FATHER OF THE BLUES

When W.C. Handy wrote his autobiography in 1941, he called himself the Father of the Blues.

Few people would disagree with that assertion. Handy, who was born in Alabama and learned to play the cornet as a child, wrote "The Memphis Blues" in 1912. He followed that with "St. Louis Blues," "Yellow Dog Blues," and "Beale Street Blues." By the time of his death in 1958, he had composed more than 80 hymns, marches, and blues tunes—and had helped make the blues part of American culture. The prestigious Blues Music Awards, which are given to top blues musicians, were formerly known as the W.C. Handy Awards.

JAZZ, MAN

Even though slavery in the United States was officially outlawed by 1865, African-Americans still had to fight for freedom in many parts of the country—especially the South. Segregation was an accepted practice: There were separate schools, separate restaurants, even separate drinking fountains for blacks and whites.

Despite being treated as second-class citizens, African-Americans in New Orleans in the early 1900s were finding freedom of expression in music.

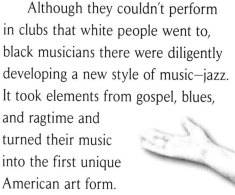

Although they couldn't perform in clubs that white people went to, black musicians there were diligently developing a new style of music—jazz. It took elements from gospel, blues, and ragtime and turned their music into the first unique American art form.

At first the only audiences for jazz were, like the musicians, black. But as the swinging beat and improvisational style spread, so did jazz's popularity among all audiences. That scared some people. There were efforts to censor what was called "devil's music." By the end of the 1920s, at least 60 cities in the United States had banned jazz in public dance halls. But no matter how hard they tried, they could not stop the spread of jazz.

Today jazz is performed and appreciated by people of all colors. Many of its musicians, such as Louis Armstrong and Ella Fitzgerald, have become larger-than-life legends. Its popularity has spread around the world. It is considered by many to be America's most important contribution to music.

Ella Fitzgerald was known as the First Lady of Song.

DOWN HOME

In the early 1920s, white singers in the Deep South and the Appalachian Mountains began incorporating the soulful sounds of the blues into their folk songs. The songs, which often included yodeled interludes and falsetto singing, were first referred to as "hillbilly" music. Later the musical style became known as country music.

Although it gained popularity as singers such as Emmett Miller and Jimmie Rodgers performed in small towns, country music really took off in 1927. That's when the Victor Talking Machine Company sent people to Bristol, Tennessee, to record the playing of local musicians. The recordings helped introduce the country sound to mainstream American audiences. The Carter Family recorded six singles one day in Bristol and went on to become country music legends.

Over the following decades, country music added sounds ranging from bluegrass and boogie-woogie to honky-tonk and rockabilly. In the 1950s, one of the best known rockabilly artists, Elvis Presley, helped establish another musical form—rock 'n' roll.

Rock 'n' roll quickly became more popular than country music, but the raw talent of singers such as Johnny Cash and Hank Williams continued to fuel the country genre. Although both artists were known as much for their hard-living lifestyles—both battled drug and alcohol addictions—as for their soulful singing, they helped blur the boundaries between country music and rock 'n' roll.

Such crossover artists have since become a mainstay, perhaps because country music includes so many forms. The diverse mix of country musicians ranges from the soulful Ray Charles and the down-home John Denver to the hard-driving Willie Nelson. In the 1990s, contemporary country singer Garth Brooks became one of the top-selling solo artists of all time with pop-country hits such as "Friends in Low Places."

Country-western legend Johnny Cash, who headlined a 1960s show in Minneapolis, Minnesota, performed until his death in 2003.

MINNEAPOLIS AUDITORIUM

SAT APR 22

SHOW 8:30 pm

Blockbuster Number 18

SMOKEY SMITH Presents

THE FABULOUS JOHNNY CASH SHOW

JUNE CARTER

THE TENN. THREE

MOTHER MAYBELLE & CARTER FAMILY

The STATLER BROS.

CARL PERKINS

TICKETS ON SALE
DOWNTOWN TICKET OFFICE - MINNEAPOLIS
FIELD SCHLICK TICKET OFFICE - ST. PAUL

EVERY SEAT RESERVED $1.50 - $3.00 - $2.50 - $2.00

15

ROCKIN' AND ROLLIN'

At first rock 'n' roll was dismissed as a fad. In an age when music was still considered black or white, and when easy, breezy pop tunes were popular, the harder-edged combination of black, white, blues, and country-western didn't seem to stand a chance. But then Bill Haley and His Comets recorded "Rock Around the Clock" and the musical landscape quickly changed. "We premiered it," Haley said in a *Rolling Stone* interview in 1967. "We put country and western together with rhythm and blues, and that was rock." It was a Number 1 hit for eight weeks and has sold more than 25 million copies worldwide. It took off after it was played during the opening credits of the 1955 film *Blackboard Jungle*.

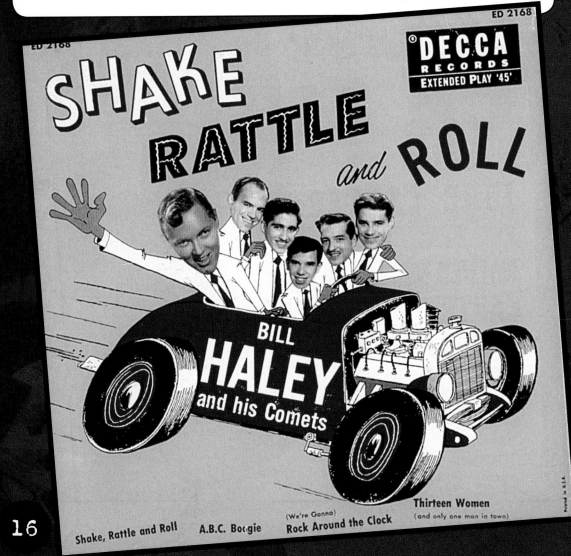

PLUGGING IN

The birth of the electric guitar changed the sound of music forever.

The Rickenbacker Company released the first version in 1931. A few years later, Les Paul developed a new solid-body electric guitar. And in 1948, Leo Fender designed the first mass-produced model, the Broadcaster. The amplified instrument, with strings that transmit electric currents through pickups, was critical to the development of jazz, blues, rock 'n' roll, country, and even some big-band music. When the Rolling Stones were inducted in the Rock and Roll Hall of Fame, guitarist Keith Richards said, "Thank God for Leo Fender, who makes these instruments for us to play."

By the mid-1950s, rock 'n' roll had both a name (coined by disc jockey Alan Freed in Cleveland, Ohio) and a growing following of fans. Bill Haley, Elvis Presley, Chuck Berry, and Little Richard were making fans scream and shout with their catchy lyrics and their hard-rocking music. Rock 'n' roll had proved that it was more than just a fad. It was working its way into the social fabric of the time: In 1956 CBS' *Rock and Roll Dance Party* became the first regularly broadcast radio program in America dedicated exclusively to the genre.

Yet rock 'n' roll also had strong and vocal opponents. Some people considered it too sexual, too rebellious, and generally too corrupt for public consumption. Performers were adored by teens but detested by many parents. Elvis, who became a sensation after recording such hits as "That's Alright (Mama)" and "Jailhouse Rock," was the target of hate mail and other personal attacks, especially after he furiously moved his hips while singing on *The Ed Sullivan Show* in 1956.

Despite the opposition, rock 'n' roll continued its evolution, and it has been the background music for several generations of Americans. It grew up with the teenagers who eagerly embraced it in the 1950s and 1960s and followed that baby boomer generation into adulthood. It also spawned new genres, including heavy metal, punk, and grunge.

MOSHING TO THE BEAT

Many fans of punk rock, heavy metal, and alternative rock enjoy "moshing" to the music—jumping around and slamming into each other.

Although many fans consider it a great way to express their appreciation for the music, some bands dislike the chaotic, sometimes dangerous elements of the mosh pits. Even before a teenager in Dublin, Ireland, was crushed to death at a Smashing Pumpkins show in 1996, the band's lead singer, Billy Corgan, had criticized moshing fans in Chicago, Illinois. "I wish you'd understand that in an environment like this, it's fairly inappropriate and unfair to the rest of the people around you," he said from the stage. "I, and we, publicly take a stand against moshing!"

BRAND NAMES AND BLING

Hip-hop is more than a certain musical sound. For many artists and their fans, it's also a fashion statement that revolves around brand name clothing and layers of big, bold jewelry.

In the 1980s, hip-hop fashionistas wore bright Nike and Adidas track suits with heavy gold chains. In the 1990s, when the rap duo Kris Kross started the trend of wearing clothes backward, the big brands were Nautica, Tommy Hilfiger, and Calvin Klein. Platinum "bling" became as popular as gold. Today several hip-hop artists, including Sean "Diddy" Combs (right) and Jay-Z, have their own clothing lines.

HIP-HOP, YOU DON'T STOP

The Bronx was not the best place to grow up in the 1970s. Gangs and graffiti were common in this tough section of New York City. Young African-Americans needed a safe alternative to the dangers on the streets. They also needed to find a way to express their feelings about growing up poor and scared. Music and dancing became outlets for their emotions.

The hip-hop culture started when disc jockeys began mixing sounds from various records. Sometimes the DJs spoke over the music, too, using words to keep the crowd dancing or to share a certain message. The new style, called rapping, turned into an art form of its own.

The first rap albums were released in 1979, including *Rapper's Delight* by the Sugar Hill Gang. The lyrics of the title track helped name the genre: "hip hip hop, you don't stop." Funky beats and rhymes were part of the package, but rappers often wrote about the realities of street life, including drugs, murders, and gang activity. They told stories of oppression and social injustice.

The anger and aggression in hip-hop music and the violent actions of some of its stars threatened some people. The sexist nature of some hip-hop lyrics even became the subject of a congressional hearing in Washington, D.C., where lawmakers asked whether the words were degrading to women. But rap's danceable beat and the brutal honesty of many of the songs resonated not only with African-Americans but also with many other young people. Women were rapping; so were white groups. The hip-hop sound became so popular that by 2002, hip-hop records were outselling other kinds of rock records.

CHAPTER 2

Leaders of the Pack

No movement, rebellious or otherwise, can survive without strong, dedicated leaders who keep the cause moving forward.
The same is true in music.

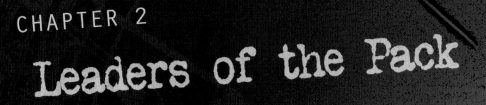

The Beatles led the "British Invasion" of the U.S. by hugely popular rock groups.

Often musical leaders have introduced new sounds and new styles to skeptical audiences. Sometimes they have caused controversy with their songs. Other times they have been pushing for the acceptance of new groups of musicians, from African-Americans to mop-haired British boys.

INNOVATORS

Musicians who try something new are innovators. They help bring new sounds to the world. Often their innovations take time to catch on. Some people prefer to avoid change and are threatened by new and different styles. Because the innovators persisted, the music they helped create became widely accepted and popular. Here is a look at some groundbreaking musicians.

JOHANN SEBASTIAN BACH

Although he was a gifted organist and composer, Johann Sebastian Bach (right) was also a troublemaker—especially with his music. In the early 1700s, the church he worked for in Germany punished him for playing too melodically and ornamentally during the hymns. When he grew tired of

working for royalty and tried to quit his job in 1717, he was arrested and thrown in jail for a month. Bach put that time to good use. He wrote 46 pieces of music while he was behind bars. Although he struggled to earn respect while he was alive, Bach is now considered one of the greatest musicians of the Baroque era. His best-known works include "Toccata and Fugue in D minor," which was used in the Disney musical film *Fantasia*. His most recognizable work, though, is "Jesu, Joy of Man's Desiring." It is often played at weddings and other religious ceremonies, usually in a slow, reverent style. (Bach's original composition, first performed in 1723, was meant to be played quickly.)

GERTRUDE "MA" RAINEY

Gertrude Pridgett was born into a family of musicians. Her parents were black minstrel show performers, and she easily accepted their way of life as her own. By the time she married William "Pa" Rainey—and became known as Ma Rainey—she was a traveling vaudeville musician herself. She was a large woman with a huge presence on stage; her hallmark was a necklace strung with 20 gold coins. Her homespun songs, including "Bo-Weevil Blues" and "C.C. Rider," described the hard country life that she—and her audiences—lived.

By the time she died of a heart attack in 1939, at age 53, Ma Rainey was known as the Mother of the Blues. She was lauded by such younger women as Lizzie Douglas (known as Memphis Minnie) and Bessie Smith as a major influence on their careers. After Rainey's death, Memphis Minnie wrote a song chronicling how the poor country girl had found fame and fortune singing the blues. In the last verse, she sang, "People sure look lonesome since Ma Rainey been gone. But she left little Minnie to carry the good works on."

LOUIS ARMSTRONG

This jazz great started life on the dirty streets of New Orleans. His neighbors were pimps, prostitutes, and gamblers. But by the time he was 21, Louis Armstrong had used his love of music to escape that life. He went to Chicago, where he played the trumpet in a jazz band. Soon he was leading his own bands and performing on his own. Although he struggled as a black man in a segregated society during his early years, he was later criticized by African-American leaders for not doing enough to help the civil rights movement of the late 1950s and 1960s. Some blacks were bothered that he played for primarily white audiences, a claim that Armstrong considered unjust. His brilliance on stage set the standard for solo jazz musicians and made him one of the greatest improvisational trumpet players in the world. "Louis Armstrong is jazz," said trumpeter Wynton Marsalis. "He represents what the music is all about."

HANK WILLIAMS

Known as the father of modern country music, Hank Williams preferred to call it honky-tonk. Mixing blues guitar riffs with heartbreaking pop lyrics about lost love and hard living, he sang with an achingly beautiful voice. He died young—at 29, the victim of alcoholism and drug abuse—just after his song "I'll Never Get Out of This World Alive" was released. His influence can still be heard in the music of country singers (including his son, Hank Williams Jr.) and rock 'n' rollers. Some of his best-known songs—"Hey Good Lookin'," "Honky Tonk Blues," and "Your Cheatin' Heart"—are considered classics today.

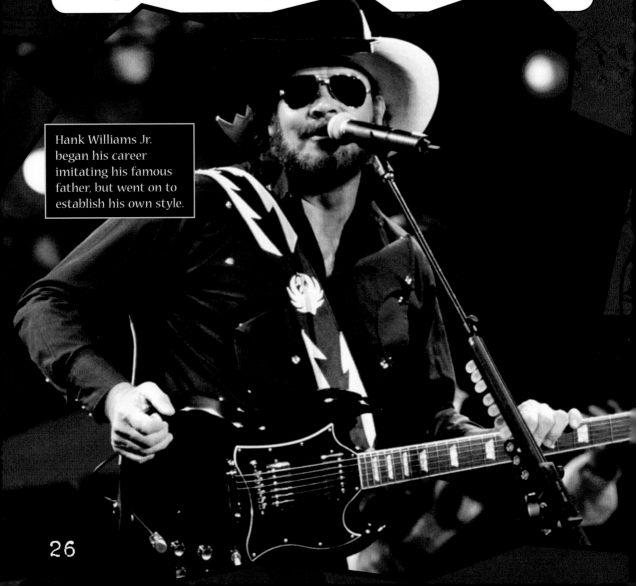

Hank Williams Jr. began his career imitating his famous father, but went on to establish his own style.

ROCK AND ROLL HALL OF FAME

Musicians, songwriters, and rock 'n' roll supporters have been inducted into the Rock and Roll Hall of Fame since 1986, but for nearly a decade there was no hall in which to honor them.

In 1995 a museum was built on the shore of Lake Erie in Cleveland—the home of disc jockey Alan Freed, who is credited with coining the term "rock 'n' roll." Janis Joplin's psychedelic-painted Porsche is part of the permanent exhibit. So are dozens of other artifacts, including rocker David Bowie's red vinyl platform boots, handwritten lyrics to songs by artists such as Jimi Hendrix and John Lennon, and even the grade school report cards of the rock duo the Everly Brothers.

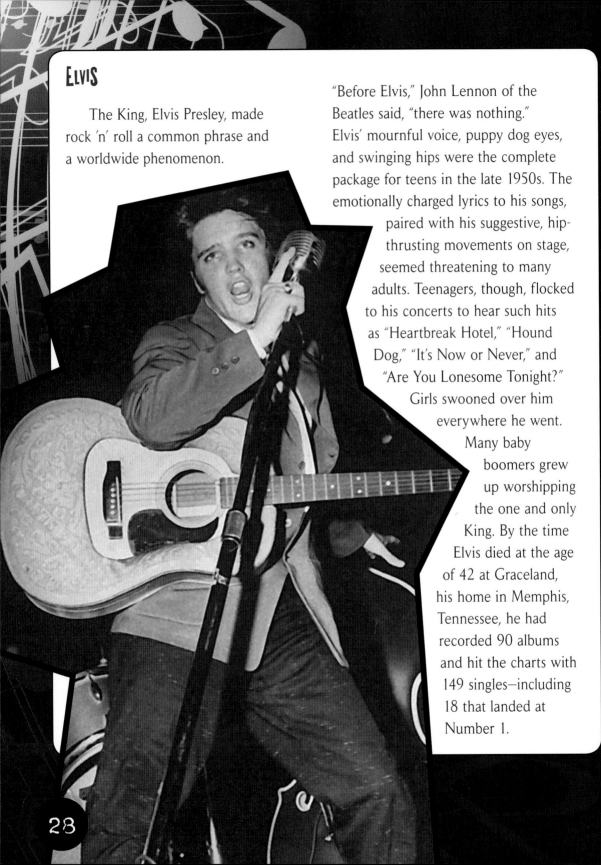

Elvis

The King, Elvis Presley, made rock 'n' roll a common phrase and a worldwide phenomenon.

"Before Elvis," John Lennon of the Beatles said, "there was nothing." Elvis' mournful voice, puppy dog eyes, and swinging hips were the complete package for teens in the late 1950s. The emotionally charged lyrics to his songs, paired with his suggestive, hip-thrusting movements on stage, seemed threatening to many adults. Teenagers, though, flocked to his concerts to hear such hits as "Heartbreak Hotel," "Hound Dog," "It's Now or Never," and "Are You Lonesome Tonight?" Girls swooned over him everywhere he went. Many baby boomers grew up worshipping the one and only King. By the time Elvis died at the age of 42 at Graceland, his home in Memphis, Tennessee, he had recorded 90 albums and hit the charts with 149 singles—including 18 that landed at Number 1.

DJ KOOL HERC

When DJ Kool Herc (Clive Campbell) set up a sound system for parties in the Bronx in the early 1970s, he liked to bring two turntables and a stack of records—many of them from funk performers such as James Brown.

He would scour his records for the most danceable beats, then use the two turntables to keep the beat going, often speaking his own words over the music to keep the crowd dancing. As he began to play at popular clubs, however, competition increased. At one point, Herc even started removing the labels from the records he spun, so spies sent by other deejays couldn't see what he was playing. Unfortunately, the hip-hop scene in the Bronx sometimes turned dangerous. Herc was stabbed three times one night, which led him to leave the party circuit for a while. Although he never became as famous as the deejays who followed him, Herc's style was the earliest form of hip-hop and has been imitated and expanded on in the decades since.

BERRY GORDY JR.

In 1959 Berry Gordy Jr. founded a Detroit, Michigan, record company that would change the face of music. It became Motown Records, and introduced audiences in America and around the world to the Motown sound—black soul music with pop appeal. In 1961 the label's "Shop Around" by the Miracles topped the *Billboard* R&B charts. By 1966 about 75 percent of the records released by Motown had hit the national charts—an astonishing figure that proved the label had successfully elevated black musicians into mainstream popularity. Gordy assembled what may be the most impressive roster of artists from a single company, all of whom have been inducted into the Rock and Roll Hall of Fame: the Four Tops, Marvin Gaye, the Jackson 5, Gladys Knight and the Pips, Martha and the Vandellas, Smokey Robinson, the Supremes, the Temptations, and Stevie Wonder. Berry Gordy himself was inducted in 1988.

Berry Gordy Jr. in front of Motown's first headquarters, Hitsville U.S.A.

AGITATORS

Agitators stir the pot. They are—by the nature of their actions, words, and works—controversial. They make people think about things in a different way. Sometimes they even help change attitudes or bring about new ways of doing things.

WOLFGANG AMADEUS MOZART

By the time he was 4 years old in 1760, Wolfgang Amadeus Mozart was making music. By the age of 6, he was making money with his music. Although he was brilliant, he was not always easy to work with. He wanted to do things his own way and was often rude and sometimes obnoxious to people. He was happiest when he was writing music, which he did with great abandon until a sudden illness led to his early death at the age of 35. Some reports suggest that even as he lay dying, he was working to complete one final work, his *Requiem Mass*. Mozart's body of work includes more than 600 compositions, including the operas *The Marriage of Figaro* and *The Magic Flute*, and many symphonies, piano sonatas, and concertos. Many of his works are considered the greatest of their kind.

A young Mozart played the harpsichord for guests at a tea in Paris in 1766.

Bob Dylan

Peace, equality, and social justice—the issues that mattered most to him—were often the subjects of Bob Dylan's lyrics. Although his songs didn't endear him to many conservatives, they did appeal to young Americans who, like Dylan, were ready for change. From the 1960s on, Dylan often used his platform to make statements about social issues.

His songs "Blowin' in the Wind" and "The Times They Are A-Changin'" have become anthems for generations of social and political activists. Dylan is best known for his poetic lyrics, his ever-present harmonica, and, until the mid-1960s, the acoustic guitar he slung over his shoulder. Then rock 'n' roll bands like The Beatles and The Byrds inspired Dylan to go electric—which the purists in the audience at the 1965 Newport Folk Festival weren't happy about. Dylan was booed off the stage after playing three "plugged in" songs. He returned to finish the set with an acoustic guitar, and for the next few years, the first half of Dylan's concerts were acoustic and the second half electric. Whichever guitar he played, he was respected most for his lyrics. "Bob freed your mind the way Elvis freed your body," said rocker Bruce Springsteen. "To this day, wherever great rock music is being made, there is the shadow of Bob Dylan."

TUPAC SHAKUR

Like many hip-hop artists, Tupac Shakur grew up in poverty, surrounded by gang violence. He used that background to write raw, emotionally charged rap songs about his hardships and to share his opinions about politics, economics, and social issues. Although his lyrics were often controversial, Tupac became the top selling hip-hop artist in the world. His hits included "Hit 'Em Up," a hard-hitting anthem that laid out the conflict between East and West Coast rappers, and "California Love," a party song with an infectious beat. He also sang a tender ode to his single mother in "Dear Mama." His death was as violent as some of his music: He died after being shot six times in a drive-by shooting in Las Vegas, Nevada, in 1996. He was 25 years old.

LIVING HARD, DYING YOUNG

The fame and fortune that come with successful musical careers have a dark side, too.

Many young stars have been seduced by the rock 'n' roll lifestyle—and many have been undone by its vices. Janis Joplin, a visionary singer and songwriter, died of a drug overdose in 1970, at the age of 27. Jim Morrison, the lead singer of The Doors, died in 1971 after battling alcohol and drug problems. He was 27. Nirvana front man Kurt Cobain was found dead of an apparent suicide in 1994. He, too, was just 27, and had struggled with drug and alcohol addictions.

AGENTS OF CHANGE

Sometimes change is slow in coming. Still, when artists with extraordinary talent who connect to a particular audience come on the scene, change often comes with them. Sometimes they seem like overnight successes—but often they owe their quick rises to stardom to the innovators and agitators who came before them.

TAKING A STAND

In early 1939, the Daughters of the American Revolution refused to allow African-American opera singer Marian Anderson to sing at Constitution Hall, a building they owned in Washington.

The service organization for descendants of people involved in the Revolutionary War had a "no blacks allowed" policy. First Lady Eleanor Roosevelt promptly resigned from the group and helped arrange for a concert at the Lincoln Memorial. Anderson's Easter Sunday concert drew a huge crowd and was broadcast throughout the country. The DAR later allowed Anderson to sing at Constitution Hall, which she did several times.

JOAN BAEZ

Joan Baez began her career as a teenager singing folk songs in coffeehouses. By the time she was 20, the dark-haired beauty with a stunning soprano voice had released her first album and found an appreciative audience for her music. Crusading for civil rights and social justice quickly became part of her career.

Even as Baez was finding commercial success, she was battling racial slurs based on her Mexican heritage (her physicist father was born in Mexico) and roadblocks based on her social activism. In 1967 she was denied the right to perform at Constitution Hall in Washington, D.C., which belongs to a patriotic service group, the Daughters of the American Revolution. DAR members did not approve of Baez's protests against the war in Vietnam.

That didn't stop Baez. She gave a free concert for 30,000 people at the Washington Monument.

Baez was such a vocal participant in protests that she was often arrested and put in jail. She even withheld part of her income taxes as a protest against the war.

Among her best-known songs are "Diamonds and Rust" and her cover of The Band's "The Night They Drove Old Dixie Down." She remains an activist for peace, human rights, and environmental preservation.

Joan Baez performed during Martin Luther King Jr.'s famous March on Washington in 1963.

THE BEATLES

Rock 'n' roll was alive and well in the United States when the Beatles came over from Great Britain. Their pop tunes quickly became successful, and American girls fell in love with the mop-topped Brits and their bright, singable songs: "I Want to Hold Your Hand," "She Loves You," "Can't Buy Me Love," and "Love Me Do."

MURDER OF JOHN LENNON

The evening of December 8, 1980, John Lennon signed a copy of his album *Double Fantasy* for a fan named Mark David Chapman.

Then, just hours later, Chapman shot the former Beatle and legendary singer and songwriter as he entered his New York City apartment building. Lennon was hit by four bullets and died before reaching a hospital. He has been mourned by millions of fans around the world, including many musicians who admired his work. Singer Elton John wrote the ballad "Empty Garden (Hey Hey Johnnie)" as a tribute to Lennon. Chapman remains in New York's Attica state prison.

As The Beatles became more successful, their message became more edgy (consider "Helter Skelter" and "While My Guitar Gently Weeps"). They evolved from a group of sunny singers to leaders of the rock 'n' roll revolution in the 1960s and early 1970s. Not only did they achieve monumental commercial success—in 1964, they claimed all five of the top spots on the *Billboard* Hot 100 list—they also helped pave the way for other British bands looking for an audience in America. The "British Invasion" brought over such rock groups as the Hollies, Freddie and the Dreamers, Wayne Fontana and the Mindbenders, the Yardbirds, the Kinks, Herman's Hermits, and the Rolling Stones. Although each group found fame and fortune in North America, none duplicated the success of The Beatles.

WILLIE NELSON

Country music superstar Willie Nelson's first impact was as a songwriter in the 1960s. He wrote songs that helped build the careers of such country legends as Patsy Cline and Roy Orbison. Cline's beautiful rendition of Nelson's "Crazy" reached Number 2 on the country charts and Number 9 on the pop charts. When the time was right (and after he had spent the first few years of the 1970s as a pig farmer), Nelson started writing songs for himself. His rebellious, anti-establishment pieces incorporated folk, rock, jazz, and country influences: "Bloody Mary Morning," "Angel Flying Too Close to the Ground," and "On the Road Again." By the mid-1970s, he was a household name—although his reputation was based as much on his rebellious attitude and his long, braided red hair as on his musical ability.

MICHAEL JACKSON

Michael Jackson was just 5 years old when he started performing with his brothers as part of the Jackson 5—an R&B pop group that got its start with Motown in 1968. From the beginning, the songs he and his four brothers recorded were hits—"I'll Be There," "ABC," and "I Want You Back." But it was as a solo artist that Jackson had the most success. *Thriller*, a multihit album released in 1982, became the best-selling album of all time and helped cement Jackson's position as the King of Pop.

As much as fans loved to hear Jackson sing, they loved to watch him dance, too. He introduced the moonwalk to his fans and seemed almost magical as he slid across the stage, bending, bouncing, and posing in perfect time to his music. As he grew older, Jackson seemed intent on shedding his little-angel image by releasing an album titled *Bad* with edgier singles, including "Dirty Diana" and "The Way You Make Me Feel." Health problems, scandals, bizarre behavior, and legal troubles sent Jackson into relative seclusion later in his career. Yet at the time of his unexpected death at age 50 in June 2009, he was preparing for a world tour that included 50 sold-out performances.

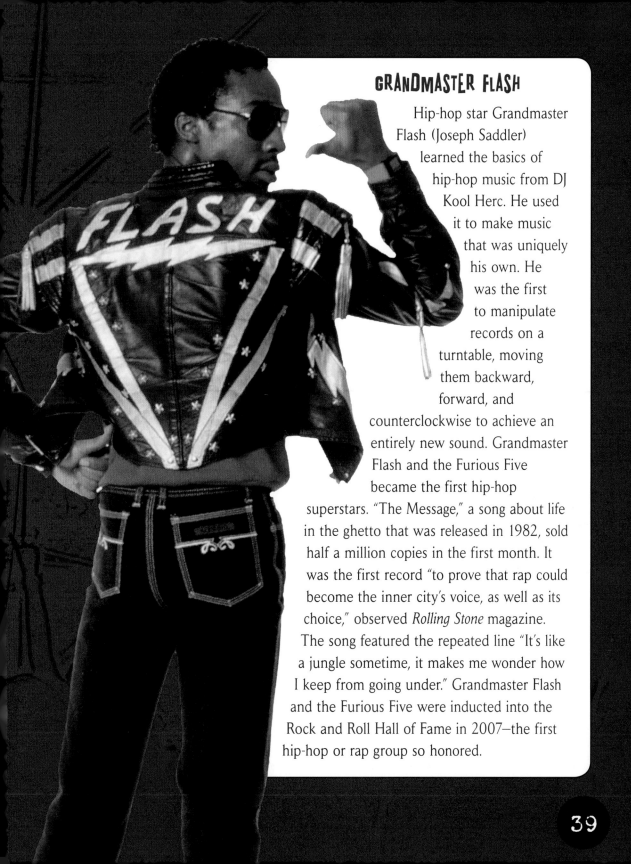

GRANDMASTER FLASH

Hip-hop star Grandmaster Flash (Joseph Saddler) learned the basics of hip-hop music from DJ Kool Herc. He used it to make music that was uniquely his own. He was the first to manipulate records on a turntable, moving them backward, forward, and counterclockwise to achieve an entirely new sound. Grandmaster Flash and the Furious Five became the first hip-hop superstars. "The Message," a song about life in the ghetto that was released in 1982, sold half a million copies in the first month. It was the first record "to prove that rap could become the inner city's voice, as well as its choice," observed *Rolling Stone* magazine. The song featured the repeated line "It's like a jungle sometime, it makes me wonder how I keep from going under." Grandmaster Flash and the Furious Five were inducted into the Rock and Roll Hall of Fame in 2007—the first hip-hop or rap group so honored.

BEAUTY OF BREAK DANCING

Just as rap and hip-hop music grew out of the inner city, so did the dance craze that went with it: break dancing.

As DJs mixed music and rappers added rhymes, fans of the new style of music dropped to the floor, kicked their legs, spun on their heads, and twisted their bodies. Many of the break-dancers who helped create the moves in the early 1980s are still doing them. "How many other dances have been created over the past 25 years that have survived this long?" says a dancer known as Crazy Legs. "It's a true American art form."

NIRVANA

Alternative rock, the work of independent, underground musicians, was just that before Nirvana—alternative. But when the Seattle-based band released "Smells Like Teen Spirit" in 1991, it suddenly became hard rock grunge. It smelled like success, too. Within two months, "Teen Spirit" was in the Top 40 and alternative rock was exploding into the mainstream. Nirvana was considered the leader of the movement, and singer and guitarist Kurt Cobain was called the "spokesman of a generation." Although his angst-ridden lyrics resonated with college students, songs such as "Come as You Are" both startled and scared older adults. Lyrics about guns and death seemed particularly troublesome after Cobain, who had battled drug addiction, committed suicide in 1994.

CHAPTER 3

Musical Statements

Throughout history, composers and performers have had ideas and topics they want to address musically. Although each usually has had a unique approach, most have focused on some form of social or political injustice.

The issues have ranged from freedom of artistic expression to racial equality and from world peace to helping starving children in Africa.

ARTISTIC EXPRESSION

Classical musicians were early crusaders for freedom of expression. Until the early 1800s, composers could only find financial success and public acclaim if they worked for a royal court or the church—and if they wrote music that their patrons approved of.

Ludwig van Beethoven, with his wild hair, dirty clothes, surly manner, and brilliant compositions, helped change that. He was the first well-known composer who never held an official court position, yet he became widely popular. He made it possible for classical composers to work for themselves, rather than for kings and queens and other royalty.

Modern musicians face different pressures. They have been asked to change their lyrics, their clothes, or the way they dance. In 1955 officials in Florida and California warned Elvis Presley that if he danced at all during his performances there, he would be arrested on obscenity charges. Even in the United States, where the First Amendment to the Constitution supposedly protects freedom of speech, musicians have battled censorship for years.

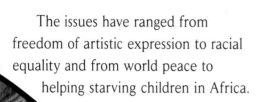

A 1750s concert in a Venetian court

Shock rocker Marilyn Manson, for example, has been banned from performing in some cities because of the disturbingly violent nature of his lyrics and his wild onstage antics. Manson's songs often include references to sex and drugs, as well as strong anti-Christian sentiments. Parents, religious groups, and lawmakers have blamed him for inciting violent acts among his fans. Despite that, Manson hasn't changed his music. "People who think that I am a threat or danger to the way they bring up their children or a danger to their religion and morals should examine their upbringing," he said in an interview. "If it is so fragile that a single person like I am can be such a threat to them, then do they really believe in their teachings?"

RITE CAUSES A RIOT

Igor Stravinsky's dissonant score for the ballet *The Rite of Spring* stands as one of the musical masterpieces of the 20th century.

But the people of Paris weren't ready for it May 29, 1913, when it was first performed. Surprised by its jarring chords and the strange, sometimes violent dance moves, the crowd at the Théatre des Champs-Elysées reacted with hisses, whistles, and catcalls. By intermission, the Paris police had been called in—but they were only partly successful in restoring order to what had turned into a full-scale riot inside the theater. Stravinsky and choreographer Vaslav Nijinsky were saddened by the reaction, but they have since been hailed as visionaries for the groundbreaking work.

RACIAL EQUALITY

African-American performers revolutionized the music scene starting in the early 1900s—from blues to jazz to soul and even rock 'n' roll. Yet despite their musical successes, African-Americans in the United States still had to fight for their civil rights—and many musicians, black and white, fought with them.

Folk singer Joan Baez led almost 300,000 people who had joined the 1963 March on Washington for Jobs and Freedom in singing "We Shall Overcome." The classic African-American gospel song became the anthem of the civil rights movement. Other popular folk singers, including Bob Dylan, Peter, Paul, and Mary, and Odetta, who was known as "the voice of the civil rights movement," were there, too. So was opera singer Marian Anderson, who had earlier fought for her right to sing at Constitution Hall in Washington, D.C.

The highlight of the march was Martin Luther King Jr.'s "I Have a Dream" speech, which is considered one of the nation's greatest speeches. The march inspired R&B singer and songwriter Curtis Mayfield to write "People Get Ready," a call to rise above racism:

People get ready,
there's a train a-comin'
You don't need no baggage,
you just get on board
All you need is faith to hear
the diesels hummin'
Don't need no ticket,
you just thank the Lord

Years later black musicians were still using their words and voices to fight for racial equality. They had legally been given equal rights, but many were now mired in poverty, fighting to stay alive in the midst of gang violence. The musicians of the hip-hop generation helped champion their causes. Some tried to inspire other young black Americans to join the fight against racism. Consider these lyrics from "Fight the Power" by the rap group Public Enemy:

While the black bands sweatin'
And the rhythm rhymes rollin'
Got to give us what we want
Gotta give us what we need
Our freedom of speech is freedom or death
We got to fight the powers that be
Lemme hear you say
Fight the power

The rap group Public Enemy has been performing for more than 20 years.

47

PEACE AND POLITICS

Politics is a touchy subject. Not everyone feels the same way about it. In fact, there are people with strong feelings on opposite sides of most political issues. So it can be risky to use politics in music. Yet for musicians who feel strongly about their beliefs, it is almost impossible not to promote them, even if doing so will hurt their careers.

It happened to the Dixie Chicks, a popular country-rock band. While on tour in 2003, singer Natalie Maines, a Texas native, told an audience in London:

"Just so you know, we're ashamed the president of the United States is from Texas." Country music fans back in the States reacted strongly to Maines' criticism of President George W. Bush's plans to invade Iraq. Some fans destroyed Dixie Chicks CDs, and some radio stations stopped playing their songs. Three years later, the Chicks were back on top of the charts with *Taking the Long Way*, and they had a successful world tour. But some people still refuse to listen to their music or buy their albums.

Musicians have been making inflammatory comments for centuries. Consider Richard Wagner, a German composer in the 1800s who revolutionized the way opera is written. Unlike most composers, he wrote his own words (librettos) to go with his compositions. He was also extremely politically active and wrote many books, poems, and essays. Unfortunately, his opinions were decidedly anti-Semitic, and he blamed Jews for society's problems. Wagner's racist writings later inspired Adolf Hitler and the Nazis.

That changed many people's opinions of Wagner, even those who appreciated his work as a composer.

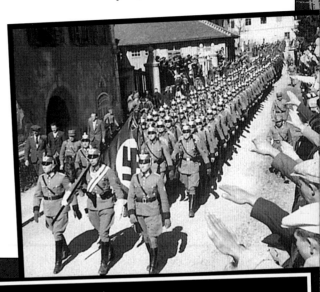

WAGNER AND THE NAZIS

German composer Richard Wagner died in 1883, six years before future Nazi dictator Adolf Hitler was born.

But because Hitler played Wagner's music at Nazi rallies, the gifted composer, who had publicly stated his own anti-Jewish views many times, became forever linked with the Holocaust that killed 6 million Jews. In Israel, the Jewish state that is home to more than 300,000 Holocaust survivors, performing Wagner's music has been unofficially banned for more than 60 years. When an Israeli orchestra broke the taboo and performed Wagner's symphonic poem "Siegfried Idyll" in 2000, protesters demonstrated outside the concert hall. Wagner's music has been performed on a few other occasions in Israel since then, but loud demonstrators have interrupted the concerts. The ban is not complete, though. Wagner's music is available on compact discs in Israel and is played on the radio.

Folk singers have often made political statements with their music. Pete Seeger was called before the House Un-American Activities Committee in 1955. He was accused of radical activism with his folk bands, primarily The Almanac Singers, which included Woody Guthrie (right). Seeger refused to answer the committee's questions and was found in contempt of Congress. Seeger, Guthrie, and many others sang about peace and social justice. They joined marches and took part in protests. In the 1960s, Bob Dylan's

opposition to the Vietnam War and support of the civil rights movement were obvious in both his music and his actions.

Those socially conscious singers

SING OUT THE VOTE

Music has been used by politicians as a rallying cry for centuries. Even George Washington had a campaign song—and he had no opponent in the first U.S. presidential election. Here are a few of the songs that became campaign tunes and the candidates who used them.

- "Follow Washington," George Washington
- "Rockabye, Baby," Martin Van Buren
- "This Land Is Your Land," George H.W. Bush
- "Don't Stop Thinking About Tomorrow," Bill Clinton
- "American Girl," Hillary Clinton

helped establish a precedent for future musicians to become activists as well. Decades later rock musicians came together to raise money for various causes, from feeding starving African children to saving American family farms. Band Aid, an effort led by Irish rocker Bob Geldof in 1984, was the first. A supergroup of Irish and British musicians released the hugely successful single "Do They Know It's Christmas?" to raise money for famine relief in Ethiopia. The following year, Michael Jackson and other musicians organized USA for Africa, also to raise money for famine relief. Their song "We Are the World" was *Billboard's* Number 1 hit of 1985.

Other collaborative efforts followed, including Farm Aid, which helped family farmers. A 1985 benefit concert was organized by Willie Nelson, Neil Young, and John Mellencamp. The Farm Aid organization continues to host yearly concerts, which have raised more than $33 million for American farmers.

The first Farm Aid concert, in Champaign, Illinois, attracted 80,000 people.

CHAPTER 4

The Effects

The sheer amount of music listened to and enjoyed today illustrates its impact on society. Classical composers, including Mozart and Beethoven, are still admired. Blues and jazz continue to be performed around the world. Rock 'n' roll and all of its many offshoots, from heavy metal to punk and grunge, are alive and well. New artists and new sounds are introduced almost every year.

Music would not have grown and developed without the contributions of musical rebels from generations past. Music is so woven into the cultural fabric of the world that the music industry generates more than $30 billion a year in sales worldwide. Many musicians are multimillionaires. Some use their wealth to make a difference in the world; others use their celebrity status to raise money for their favorite causes.

Musical innovations have helped launch other innovations as well, particularly in the recording industry. To keep up with the variety and quantity of music being made—and to satisfy consumers' demands for high-quality recordings—new technology had to be created. Records, eight-track tapes, and tape cassettes were all at one time considered groundbreaking technology. Now even compact discs, which amazed listeners with their clean, pure sounds when first released in 1982, are at risk of becoming obsolete. More and more consumers choose to download music. By the end of 2008, sales of compact discs were declining, while sales of digital music during the year totaled $3.7 billion—even though 95 percent of downloads are illegal.

The hip-hop group Black Eyed Peas has sold more than 29 million albums.

RECORD OF RECORDING

1880s-1910s

PHONOGRAPH CYLINDERS

The first mass-marketed cylinders were made of wax that had audio recordings engraved on the outside surface. The sound could be reproduced by playing the cylinder on a mechanical phonograph.

1887-1990s

RECORDS

Records are an analog sound storage medium in which a flat disc is inscribed with a spiral groove that starts on the outside edge and continues winding around to the center. Although digital media began to replace records in the 1980s, records continue to be manufactured. Old records and their covers are popular collector's items.

1960s-1980s

EIGHT-TRACK TAPES

The advent of reel-to-reel recording led to eight-track tapes, which allowed magnetic sound recordings to be automatically switched between tracks. Because car manufacturers added eight-track players to their vehicles, the format was popular in cars before it entered homes.

1960s-1990s

CASSETTE TAPES

Another spin-off of reel-to-reel recording, cassette tapes are also a magnetic sound recording format. A magnetically coated plastic tape that can record sound is wound around two tiny spools held in a plastic case.

Inventor Thomas Edison recorded the words to "Mary Had a Little Lamb" on a cylinder whose contents could be played back on a phonograph. It was the first step toward bringing popular music into homes. In the years since, sound recording has been continually improved, spurred by consumer demand and technological advances.

Here's a look back:

1982–PRESENT

COMPACT DISCS

Compact discs are optical discs that can store large amounts of digital data. They were originally developed to replace records as the best way to record and store music, but they have since become popular for storing other data, including images and text. The first album released on CD was Billy Joel's *52nd Street* in 1982.

1994–PRESENT

MP3S

A patented digital audio format, MP3 recorders compress audio files so they can be downloaded quickly from the Internet. They are stored and played on computers and MP3 players, including iPods.

The evolution of music has changed the mass media as well. Music's role in society has spawned dozens of popular magazines, many of which have become as culturally important as the musicians and topics they document. Consider *Rolling Stone*, which has been around for more than 40 years and has become a respected source of political and social reporting as well as music journalism. Entire television networks have been built around music, including MTV and VH1, which have been airing music videos and musically themed programs since the early 1980s.

MTV, with its VJs playing music videos, was launched in 1981.

All of that public exposure has helped more people become aware of the variety of music—and has helped spread the social messages that are so often part of music. And it helps bring about the kind of change that many musicians are hoping for. Jay-Z (below), a rapper and record producer, believes that the spread of hip-hop music around the world has gone a long way toward achieving racial equality. "Rap music has done more for racial equality than any other personality or element has done," he said in an interview in *Fortune* magazine. "Racism, hatred, starts in the home, at a young age. But it's hard to really teach hatred when your kid has a picture of Snoop Dogg on the wall."

Performers and other musical artists who were once criticized, shunned, and rejected have since gained acceptance and, in many cases, respect. Many are still performing—even aging bands such as the

Rolling Stones, whose lead singer, Mick Jagger, is now a grandfather. Some have brought new generations of rebels into the industry. Bob Dylan's son Jakob, for example, has a successful singing career of his own—while his father continues to tour and record music.

Top Sellers

Here are the best-selling U.S. albums of all time:

- *Thriller*, Michael Jackson
- *The Eagles, Their Greatest Hits 1971–1975*, The Eagles
- *Led Zeppelin IV*, Led Zeppelin
- *The Wall*, Pink Floyd
- *Back in Black*, AC/DC
- *Double Live*, Garth Brooks
- *Greatest Hits Volumes I and II*, Billy Joel
- *Come on Over*, Shania Twain
- *The Beatles*, The Beatles
- *Rumours*, Fleetwood Mac

As reported by the Recording Industry Association of America

Today's musical rebels continue to test the limits musically and socially. Many are inspired by rebels from the past, and they often try to push the boundaries even further. Actions like Elvis' gyrating hips, which were so disturbing in the 1950s that some television cameras were focused only on his face and torso, had become acceptable by the 1980s. Madonna started new controversies with the seductive dance moves she used during songs such as "Like a Virgin" and "Material Girl." But by the mid-1990s, those moves were not only being imitated but also taken to a new level by the next generation of singers, including Britney Spears.

WOODSTOCK
MUSIC & ART FAIR
presents
AN
AQUARIAN
EXPOSITION
in
WHITE LAKE, N.Y.

3 DAYS of PEACE & MUSIC

AUGUST 15, 16, 17

Music's rebellious history is far from over. Just as music has evolved over the past centuries, it will continue changing for centuries to come. Every new generation faces, and helps to bring about, social, political, and cultural changes. Music has long been the voice of those changes. It has become a universal language that can be used and understood by everyone, regardless of race, gender, ethnicity, or nationality.

It will continue to raise questions, challenge tradition, and change the social fabric of society—just as Bob Dylan predicted decades ago:

As the present now
Will later be past
The order is
Rapidly fadin'.
And the first one now
Will later be last
For the times they are a-changin'.

Timeline

600 ············· Gregorian chants are written

1430 ············· The Renaissance begins; the popularity of secular music increases

1807 ············· Beethoven completes his Symphony No. 5, which many consider the most popular classical work ever written

1877 ············· Thomas Edison invents sound recording; he patents the phonograph the next year

1922 ············· Jazz pianist Jelly Roll Morton and trumpeter Louis Armstrong arrive in Chicago, and the Midwestern city becomes the new capital of jazz

1931 ············· The electric guitar is introduced

1958 ············· *Billboard* debuts its Hot 100 chart, with Ricky Nelson's "Poor Little Fool" as the first Number 1 record

1963 ············· Beatlemania erupts in England and Europe; the following year The Beatles take the U.S. by storm

1979 ············· The Sugar Hill Gang releases the first commercial rap hit, "Rapper's Delight," bringing rap off the New York streets and into popular music

1981 ············· MTV begins

1984 ············· Band Aid releases "Do They Know It's Christmas?" with proceeds helping to feed starving people in Africa

1991 ············· Nirvana releases "Smells Like Teen Spirit," launching the grunge movement

2002 ············· Hip-hop albums outsell rock albums for the first time

2009 ············· Downloads of Michael Jackson's music set a record after his unexpected death at age 50

Glossary

activist	person who works for social or political change
anthem	song used in celebration or recognition of a country, idea, or institution
censor	to remove or prohibit words or actions thought to be politically or morally objectionable
civil rights	person's rights that are guaranteed by the U.S. Constitution
disc jockey	announcer, also called a deejay, who plays and comments on recorded music on the radio or at a party
dissonant	not in harmony; harsh
fad	style or movement that interests a large group of people for a short time
genre	category of music, literature, and art characterized by a particular style, form, or content
graffiti	pictures or words drawn or painted on walls and other surfaces, usually without permission
improvisational	composed without preparation, usually while performing
lyrics	words to a song
pickups	devices that capture mechanical vibrations from string instruments and convert them to electrical signals, which can be amplified
segregation	practice of separating people of different races
turntable	record player

Additional Resources

Bertholf, Bret. *The Long Gone Lonesome History of Country Music*. New York: Little, Brown and Co., 2007.

Freedman, Russell. *The Voice That Challenged a Nation: Marian Anderson and the Struggle for Equal Rights*. New York: Clarion Books, 2004.

Gourse, Leslie. *Sophisticated Ladies: The Great Women of Jazz*. New York: Dutton Children's Books, 2007.

Kallen, Stuart A. *The History of Classical Music*. San Diego: Lucent Books, 2003.

Krull, Kathleen. *Lives of the Musicians: Good Times, Bad Times (And What the Neighbors Thought)*. San Diego: Harcourt, 2002.

Partridge, Elizabeth. *John Lennon: All I Want Is the Truth*. New York: Viking, 2005.

Partridge, Elizabeth. *This Land Was Made for You and Me: The Life and Songs of Woody Guthrie*. New York: Viking, 2002.

Weatherford, Carole Boston. *Becoming Billie Holiday*. Honesdale, Pa.: Wordsong, 2008.

Weller, Sheila. *Girls Like Us: Carole King, Joni Mitchell, Carly Simon–And the Journey of a Generation*. New York: Atria Books, 2008.

FactHound

FactHound offers a safe, fun way to find Internet sites related to this book. All of the sites on FactHound have been researched by our staff.

Here's all you do:
Visit *www.facthound.com*
FactHound will fetch the best sites for you!

Look for the other books in this series:

GAMERS UNITE!
The Video Game Revolution

YOU CAN'T READ THIS!
Why Books Get Banned

GRAPHIC CONTENT!
The Culture of Comic Books

Select Bibliography

Abrams, Jim. "House Panel Debates Hip-Hop Lyrics." *The Washington Post*. 25 Sept. 2007. 27 July 2009. www.washingtonpost.com/wp-dyn/content/article/2007/09/25/AR2007092500908.html

American Masters: Louis Armstrong. PBS. 27 July 2009. www.pbs.org/wnet/americanmasters/episodes/louis-armstrong/about-louis-armstrong/528/

Culture Shock. Flashpoints: Music and Dance. 27 July 2009. www.pbs.org/wgbh/cultureshock/flashpoints/index.html

Davis, Francis. *The History of the Blues*. Cambridge, Mass.: Da Capo Press, 2003.

"Dylan Goes Electric in 1965: 50 moments that changed the history of rock & roll." *Rolling Stone*. 24 June 2004. 27 July 2009. www.rollingstone.com/news/story/6085476/dylan_goes_electric_in_1965

Egan, Sean, ed. *Defining Moments in Music: The Greatest Artists, Albums, Songs, Performances and Events That Rocked the Music World*. London: Cassell Illustrated, 2007.

Essentials of Music. 27 July 2009. www.essentialsofmusic.com

Eylon, Lili. "The Controversy Over Richard Wagner." Jewish Virtual Library. 29 July 2009. www.jewishvirtuallibrary.org/jsource/anti-semitism/Wagner.html

Glennon, James. *Understanding Music*. New York: St. Martin's Press, 1980.

Palmer, Robert. *Rock & Roll: An Unruly History*. New York: Harmony Books, 1995.

Rock and Roll Hall of Fame and Museum. 27 July 2009. www.rockhall.com

Ward, Geoffrey C. *Jazz: A History of America's Music*. New York: Alfred A. Knopf, 2000.

Wenner, Jann S. "Our 1000th Issue: Jann Wenner looks back on 39 years of *Rolling Stone*." *Rolling Stone*. 4 May 2006. 27 July 2009. www.rollingstone.com/news/story/10224178/our_1000th_issue

Wilford, John Noble. "Flutes Offer Clues to Stone-Age Music." *The New York Times*. 24 June 2009. 27 July 2009. www.nytimes.com/2009/06/25/science/25flute.html

Wormser, Richard. *The Birth of the Blues (1900–10)*. PBS. 27 July 2009. www.pbs.org/wnet/jimcrow/stories_events_blues.html

Index

About the Author

Sara Gilbert studied journalism at the University of St. Thomas in St. Paul, Minnesota, and intended to find her first job writing for *Rolling Stone* magazine. She still hasn't gotten that gig, but she has been writing magazine stories, newspaper articles, and books for more than 15 years. She juggles a freelance writing career with taking care of her three children, Ben, Jack, and Lucy. She and her husband, Shane, live in Mankato, Minnesota.